Teemu
Selanne

KERRY BANKS

GREYSTONE BOOKS
Douglas & McIntyre
Vancouver/Toronto/New York

Text copyright © 1999 by Kerry Banks

99 00 01 02 5 4 3 2 1

Greystone Books
A division of Douglas & McIntyre Ltd.
2323 Quebec Street, Suite 201
Vancouver, British Columbia
Canada V5T 4S7

Canadian Cataloguing in Publication Data
Banks, Kerry, 1952–
    Teemu Selanne
    (Hockey heroes)
    ISBN 1-55054-678-3
    1. Selanne, Teemu—Juvenile literature. 2. Hockey players—Biography—
Juvenile literature. I. Title. II. Series: Hockey heroes (Vancouver, B.C)
GV848.5.S44B36 1999   j796.962'092   C99-910172-2

Editing by Michael Carroll
Cover and text design by Peter Cocking
Front cover photograph by Bruce Bennett/Bruce Bennett Studios
Back cover photograph by John Tremmel/Bruce Bennett Studios
Printed and bound in Canada by Friesens on acid-free paper ∞

The publisher gratefully acknowledges the assistance of the Canada Council for the Arts and of the British Columbia Ministry of Tourism, Small Business and Culture. The publisher also acknowledges the financial support of the Government of Canada through the Book Publishing Industry Development Program for its publishing activities.

Canadä

Photo credits
Photos by Bruce Bennett Studios:
pp. i (top), 9, 10, 18,
21, 39: Bruce Bennett
pp. i (center left),
13, 17, 25: Tony Biegun
pp. i (center right),
33: John Giamundo
p. i (bottom): John Tremmel
pp. iii, 34: Henry DiRocco
pp. iv, 3, 30: Robert Laberge
pp. 6, 29: Mark Hicks
p. 26: Claus Andersen
p. 36: Brian Winkler
p. 40: Art Foxall
p. 43: Brian McCormick

Photos by Lehtikuva:
p. 5: Matti Björkman
p. 14: Heikki Saukkomaa
p. 22: Markku Ulander

JETTING TO THE TOP 11

WINDS OF CHANGE 19

NEW DUCK ON THE POND 27

CARRYING THE LOAD 35

STATISTICS 44

One of the NHL's fastest

and most explosive

skaters, Teemu creates

serious trouble for

opposing defenders in

open ice.

CHAPTER ONE

The Finnish Flash

The fans at Madison Square Gardens were whooping it up. The hometown New York Rangers led the Anaheim Mighty Ducks 3–1 in the third period and were dominating play. Then, suddenly, things changed. Ducks right winger Teemu Selanne took a breakaway pass, streaked in on goalie Mike Richter, made a deke and put the puck in the corner of the net. Minutes later, with the two teams playing four a side, Teemu pounced on a loose puck in his own zone. With a burst of speed, he swept around one Ranger, stickhandled past another, then split the defense and rifled a shot past Richter. The goal—Teemu's third of the game—tied the score and silenced the noisy New York crowd.

It was a spectacular goal that only a handful of players in the world could have scored. Unfortunately for the Rangers, Teemu is one of those players. Known as one of the most feared marksmen in the National Hockey League, the Finnish forward can turn a game around in an instant.

Like most top guns, Teemu has a hard, accurate shot and a lightning-quick release. Give him a chance near the net and he rarely misses. As his linemate Paul Kariya says: "Some players are natural goal scorers. They have a touch with the puck. Teemu has the touch."

But beyond his scoring touch, what sets Teemu apart is his ability to play the game at high tempo. Nicknamed the "Finnish Flash" because of his blinding speed, he can

Teemu knows

you have to pay the

price to score.

take a pass in full stride, fight off a defender and get into shooting position, all without slowing down. He is also a clever player with sharp hockey instincts, and at six feet (1.83 meters) and 200 pounds (91 kilograms), he is stronger than many NHL snipers.

Yet, while Teemu may be pure poison for his opponents, he is one of the sweeter players off the ice. Always upbeat and smiling, he inspires a special affection in teammates and fans alike. Ron Wilson, his former coach in Anaheim, once noted: "I think the epitaph on Teemu's

tombstone is going to read: 'I had a million friends and not one enemy.' He's a guy you just love being around."

Fitting for an unusual player, Teemu had an unusual beginning. He and his twin brother, Paavo, were born moments apart on July 3, 1970, in Helsinki, Finland's capital. Teemu's dad, Ilmari, was an engineer and his mother, Liisa, was a schoolteacher. They loved the outdoors, and all the boys, including Teemu and Paavo's older brother, Panu, were encouraged to play sports.

Teemu learned to skate at age five. As a youngster, he closely followed the career of his countryman, Jari Kurri, who rose to stardom with the Edmonton Oilers. Teemu, who was a big Oilers fan, had pictures of Kurri and Wayne Gretzky on his bedroom wall.

At 12 Teemu traveled to Canada with his local team to play in the Esso Challenge Cup tournament in Toronto. During the trip, his father bought him an Oilers jersey with Kurri's name and number (17) on the back. When he returned home, Teemu wore his treasured sweater everywhere. He still has it.

Teemu was also a talented soccer player. But hockey was the sport he loved best, mostly because of its

Jokers Wild

Jokerit Helsinki, the hockey team that Teemu Selanne played for in Finland, was founded in 1967. The club was named after its sponsor, a paint company that had just developed a new product called Joker Paint. The paint, which was blended with water rather than oil, was an instant success because it had fewer fumes and was quick to dry. The company logo is modeled after the image of a joker in a deck of playing cards. It's the symbol the team wears on its sweaters. Other Jokerit players who have played in the NHL include Jari Kurri, Janne Niinimaa and Juha Lind.

speed. Going fast was always an attraction for Teemu, who is a bit of a daredevil. When he was a teenager, he and his friends would drive down to the frozen ocean. Then they would put on skates, tie ropes to a car bumper and hang on as it pulled them across the thick ice.

Hockey became Teemu's main focus at age 17 when he joined the Finnish national junior team. "That's when I decided to see how far I could go. At that time, the NHL wasn't a realistic goal for me. My goal was to play in the top Finnish league, make the national team and play in the Olympics."

Teemu first made headlines in 1987–88 with the Jokerit Helsinki junior team when he scored a sizzling 43 goals and 23 assists for 66 points in just 33 games. At the season's end, he was moved up to Jokerit's senior squad, which was playing in Finland's Second Division.

Helsinki hockey fans weren't the only ones impressed by Teemu's skills. NHL scouts were watching his progress because he was eligible for the 1988 NHL Entry Draft. Many felt he was the best European player available. Some even thought he was the best player overall. If Teemu had been a Canadian junior, he would have been one of the first

three picks. But because he was a European he was considered a riskier choice. Teemu was eventually taken 10th overall by the Winnipeg Jets.

Unlike the other top prospects, Teemu didn't attend the Entry Draft. But he had a good excuse. He had just been selected in another draft at home—by the Finnish army. All young men in Finland must spend a year in the military. Teemu began his service in the summer of 1988.

In 1988–89, his first full season with Jokerit's senior team, Teemu had a terrific year, scoring 35 goals and 33 assists for 68 points in 34 games. Jokerit finished first and earned a promotion into Finland's top league. The next season, Teemu eagerly set out to test himself against Finland's best players. His excitement was short-lived. In the 11th game of the season, he suffered a broken leg. It took a year to heal.

But Teemu recovered. In 1990–91, he had another fine season, posting 33 goals and 25 assists for 58 points in 42 games. When the season ended, he joined the Finnish national

THE TEEMU SELANNE FILE

Position: Right wing
Born: July 3, 1970, Helsinki, Finland
Height: Six feet (1.83 meters)
Weight: 200 pounds (91 kilograms)
Shoots: Right
Number: 8
Nicknames: The Finnish Flash, Salami
Favorite Food: Reindeer steak

Hobbies: Playing guitar, magic tricks, racing cars
Off-Season Sports: Water skiing, sailing, tennis
Childhood Hockey Heroes: Jari Kurri, Wayne Gretzky, Guy Lafleur
Hockey Highlight: Breaking Mike Bossy's rookie goal-scoring record

team for the World Championships. After the tournament, Winnipeg Jets general manager Mike Smith attempted to sign the young Finn to an NHL contract. But Teemu said no. He had two more things he wanted to do before joining the NHL: win a championship with Jokerit and play at the 1992 Olympics.

In 1991–92, Teemu achieved both those dreams. He scored 39 goals and 23 assists for 62 points and led Jokerit to the league championship. He also played for his country at the Winter Olympics. Although he scored seven goals and added four assists in eight games, Finland didn't win a medal.

Again, Smith tried to sign Teemu to a contract, but there was a complication. Because he hadn't been signed in three years, Teemu was now a free agent. That meant other teams could bid for his services. If he accepted any of their offers, Winnipeg would have to match it or lose their rights to him.

Teemu's dream was to wear Finland's national colors.

The Calgary Flames quickly offered Teemu a three-year contract at $400,000 a year. To sweeten the deal, they included a $1.5-million signing bonus. When Teemu signed the Flames' offer sheet, the Jets were on the spot. Reluctantly Smith matched. The deal made Teemu one of the NHL's highest-paid players before he played a single game in the pros.

Teemu's decision to join the NHL didn't go over well in his native land. The day he left, a crowd gathered at the Helsinki airport to say goodbye. Many people cried. It was a sad day in Finland.

Teemu has so many different moves that goalies are never sure what he is going to do with the puck.

CHAPTER TWO

Jetting to the Top

Teemu who? That's what many sportswriters were asking when they heard about the big contract the Finnish rookie had signed with the Winnipeg Jets. Because of that contract, Teemu would be expected to make a splash. But few rookies are able to step right into an NHL lineup. It's an even tougher chore for Europeans because they have to adjust to a smaller rink, a longer schedule, a tougher brand of hockey and a new culture.

Still, Teemu had a few advantages. At 22 he was older than most rookies. Besides, the Jets played a free-wheeling style that suited his game. The team also had a strong European flavor, with four Russians, two Swedes and another Finn, defenseman Teppo Numminen.

Teemu began the season on an all-rookie line with center Alexei Zhamnov and left winger Darrin Shannon. He picked up an assist on Winnipeg's first goal of the season as the Jets defeated the Detroit Red Wings 4–1. He notched his first NHL goal in his second game, firing a bullet past goalie Jeff Hackett in a 4–3 loss to the San Jose Sharks.

But it was in his fifth game that the Finnish rookie showed his true potential, potting three goals as the Jets thumped the Edmonton Oilers 7–4. Teemu soon began scoring in bunches. He hit for another hat trick on December 11 versus the Washington Capitals. By the end of December, he had scored 30 goals in 38 games. Images of Teemu zipping past defensemen and deking goalies out of their underwear were now a regular feature of the nightly television highlights.

Teemu celebrates

the goal that broke

Mike Bossy's record.

Teemu's play was so impressive that he received more votes than any other right winger in the mid-season All-Star voting. Yet, as well as he had performed in the first half, many hockey experts predicted that Teemu's production would tail off. But he surprised everyone by getting stronger as the year wore on.

By late February, the Finn was closing in on Mike Bossy's NHL rookie record of 53 goals, set in 1977–78. On February 28, he blew past the 50-goal mark in dramatic style, scoring four

times in a 7–6 win over the Minnesota North Stars (now the Dallas Stars). Teemu had scored 51 goals in just 63 games.

In his next game, on March 2, at Winnipeg Arena, Teemu shattered Bossy's record. He did it with flair, scoring three times against the Quebec Nordiques (now the Colorado Avalanche). His third goal, the record-breaker, came at 9:16 of the third period. Jets winger Tie Domi lofted a long pass from his own end. Teemu raced down the ice, beat goalie Stephane Fiset to the skittering puck and chipped it into the empty cage.

The Finn celebrated by wheeling around and tossing one glove high into the air. Then he picked up his stick, glided on one knee and pointed his stick like a rifle, pretending to shoot the glove out of the air. It was a move he had used on special occasions in Finland, but never before in the NHL. The Winnipeg fans cheered wildly.

The game was halted for 10 minutes, and Teemu was given a silver-plated stick by team owner Barry Shenkarow. The hoopla seemed to distract the Jets, who allowed Quebec to pump in four goals in the last 10 minutes of the game. Although the 7–4 loss was disappointing, it didn't lessen Teemu's accomplishment.

Teemu continued to score at a blistering pace. A few nights later, against the Tampa Bay Lightning, he recorded another hat trick. His third goal came on a penalty shot. When Tampa Bay goalie Wendell Young was asked later about the penalty shot, he said: "When I saw Teemu take the puck at center ice, I thought to myself, 'Okay, Wendell, kiss your butt goodbye.' All you can do is watch him with admiration and hope he makes a mistake and hits you with the puck."

On March 23, Teemu posted his 110th point and surpassed another rookie milestone: Peter Stastny's NHL record for most points in a season. Teemu racked up 20 goals in the month of March. He ended the season with a 17-game point streak,

Head of the Class

While playing hockey in Finland, Teemu Selanne also taught kindergarten for three years. The kids knew about his night job, but didn't fully understand it. "When I left for the game, they would say, 'Hey, Teemu, score a thousand goals.'" Today, Teemu still keeps in touch with his former students, who follow his career in the newspapers and on the Internet.

and the Jets surged right along with him, finishing fourth in the Pacific Division. But Winnipeg couldn't keep up its pace in the playoffs. For the second straight year, the Jets were defeated by the Vancouver Canucks.

Although Jets fans were unhappy about the club's playoff performance, no one had any complaints about the play of Winnipeg's high-priced Finnish import. Teemu's final stats were awesome. He scored 76 goals and 56 assists for 132 points, fifth best in the league. His 76 goals was the fourth-highest total in NHL history, and it tied him with the Buffalo Sabres' Alexander Mogilny for the goal-scoring lead. His 132 points broke Dale Hawerchuk's team record of 130 points. In all, he broke 14 Jets scoring records.

Teemu won the Calder Trophy as the NHL's rookie of the year in a landslide, not bad considering the competition included a kid in Philadelphia named Eric Lindros. Teemu who? No one had to ask that anymore.

R O O K I E   S N I P E R S

No rookie has ever taken the NHL by storm the way Teemu Selanne did in 1992–93. The Flying Finn didn't just break the existing rookie goal-scoring record, he demolished it.

Player	Season	Team	Goals
Teemu Selanne	1992–93	Winnipeg Jets	76
Mike Bossy	1977–78	New York Islanders	53
Joe Nieuwendyk	1987–88	Calgary Flames	51
Dale Hawerchuk	1981–82	Winnipeg Jets	45
Luc Robitaille	1986–87	Los Angeles Kings	45

Unlike some European

players, Teemu made a

smooth adjustment to the

smaller ice surface and

more physical game

in the NHL.

CHAPTER THREE

Winds of Change

Heading into the 1993–94 season, the Winnipeg Jets were optimistic. Despite an early exit in the 1993 playoffs, the team had improved on its record for the third straight season. And with Teemu Selanne, Alexei Zhamnov and Keith Tkachuk, the Jets had three of the best young forwards in the NHL.

Teemu began his second season with a bang, scoring three times as the Jets downed the Washington Capitals 6–4. Winnipeg reporters joked that Teemu was on pace to score 246 goals. But as the season progressed, it was clear the Jets lacked something. Their play was often ragged and sluggish. The team especially seemed to miss the creative talents of defenseman Phil Housley, who had been traded to St. Louis.

By Christmas, Teemu was on pace to score 45 goals, a respectable total, but less than what the Jets were hoping for. Some observers felt he lacked intensity. Mike Smith, Winnipeg's general manager, accused the young Finn of being in "dreamland." In response to the criticism, Teemu gave an interview in which he said: "Our expectations are just as high as the fans. Still, some people are looking for the moon or the sky and we aren't that good." Teemu, however, promised the team would improve and vowed he would play better in the second half.

In January, with the team still struggling, Jets owner Barry Shenkarow fired Smith and appointed coach John Paddock to take his place as general manager. Paddock quickly made a couple of trades to try to change the team's fortunes.

The Finnish Flash owns 25 Winnipeg scoring records.

On January 12, against the Buffalo Sabres, Teemu scored his 100th NHL goal. It came in his 130th game, leaving him one game short of Mike Bossy's NHL record for the fastest player to reach the century mark. When the All-Star squads were announced that month, the flashy Finn was once again voted to the team.

His appearance at the 1994 All-Star Game was Teemu's last highlight of the year. On January 26, during the second

period of a game against the Anaheim Mighty Ducks, he tried to bodycheck defenseman Don McSween, who jumped to avoid the collision. As McSween came down, his skate blade hit the exposed part of Teemu's ankle. It cut deep into his Achilles tendon, which connects the calf muscle to the heel bone.

When doctors examined the injury, they discovered that 75 per cent of the tendon had been severed. Teemu had to undergo surgery. His season was done after 51 games. He left the lineup with 26 goals and 29 assists for 54 points, tops on the team.

The loss of Teemu was a devastating blow. Winnipeg slumped badly, finishing with the second-worst record in the NHL. To make matters worse, owner Shenkarow announced

that the Jets were losing money and that unless the city built a new hockey arena he would have to sell the team.

Teemu returned to Finland after the season to recover. His first chance to test his repaired tendon came in front of his hometown fans. In September 1994, the Jets held their training camp in Finland. While there they competed in a tournament against two top Finnish teams. Teemu played well and was voted the most valuable player of the event.

However, his comeback had to be put on hold. A dispute between the NHL owners and the players' association over money caused the owners to close their arenas. The season was suspended until an agreement could be reached. During the lockout, many NHL players competed in Europe. Teemu played with Jokerit, his old Finnish team.

The lockout ended in January. Although Teemu's Achilles tendon had healed, it still wasn't 100 per cent, and he had a new problem—inflamed tendons in his knees. "It was a painful injury," he recalls. "I couldn't push down on my knees at all." Even though he wasn't at his physical peak, Teemu posted 22 goals and 26 assists in 45 games. But Winnipeg never got back on track under new coach Terry Simpson and missed the playoffs again.

The gloomy picture got darker the next month. The Manitoba government and local corporations weren't able to raise enough money to build a new arena. On May 1, Shenkarow put the club up for sale. In response, 35,000 fans held an emotional rally to save the Jets.

For the 1995–96 season, Winnipeg's management chose the slogan "A Year to Remember." Unfortunately it rapidly became

Car Crazy

Next to hockey, Teemu Selanne's biggest passion is cars. At last count, he owned 24. Most of them are powerful muscle cars from the 1960s. His collection includes a Firebird, a Camaro, a GTO and a Corvette Stingray. He also owns a Porsche, a Ferrari and a Dodge Viper. In the summer, Teemu competes in off-road races in Finland, roaring through the forest in souped-up, four-wheel-drive rally cars. He races under the name Teddy Flash. He picked the name because he was worried that if the Winnipeg Jets knew what he was doing they would object to his dangerous hobby.

a season to forget. Distracted by the uncertainty about the club's future, the Jets got off to a slow start. Then, on December 4, all hopes of saving the team vanished when the team's new owner, Jerry Colangelo, announced he would move the franchise to Phoenix at the end of the season.

Fully recovered from his physical woes, Teemu seemed determined to make his last year in Winnipeg a memorable one. On December 16, in a 9–4 win over Edmonton, he scored four times. On December 28, he began a 15-game scoring streak that lasted until February 4. He also played in his third All-Star Game, where he struck up a friendship with Paul Kariya, a dazzling young forward with the Anaheim Mighty Ducks.

When Kariya returned to Anaheim, he told Ducks general manager Jack Ferreira how much Teemu had impressed him. Little did the two players realize they would soon be seeing a lot more of each other.

BACHELOR PARTY

In July 1996, a few days before Teemu Selanne and his fiancée, Sirpa, were married, the Finnish Flash was snatched by kidnappers. They blindfolded and took him away in a van. Luckily the kidnappers were his buddies. The stunt was the start of a wild, two-day bachelor party. Before it ended, Teemu had been paraded around Helsinki dressed like Elvis Presley and had one of his ankles tattooed with a yellow lightning bolt. Later, Teemu was blindfolded again, given a change of clothes and driven around town with the van's stereo cranked up high. When the van stopped and his blindfold was removed, he found himself on a soccer field in front of 10,000 fans. He was wearing the uniform of one of Finland's top soccer teams. Seconds later, someone yelled, "Play!" So Teemu did. As he recalls: "I even shot once and hit the post. It was great."

One of the NHL's grittier finesse players, Teemu has the strength and courage to hang tough around the net.

New Duck on the Pond

As Teemu left the ice after practice on February 8, 1995, he was asked to step into the office of Jets coach Terry Simpson. There he learned that he had been traded to the Anaheim Mighty Ducks for two 19-year-olds, Chad Kilger and Oleg Tverdovsky. Moments later, he walked into the dressing room and tore his nameplate off his locker.

The news was a total shock. "Two weeks before, I had heard some trade rumors," recalls Teemu, "but the team's new owner phoned me at home and told me not to worry, that I was going to be a big part of the team's future. Then, 10 days later, bang, I'm gone." The timing of the trade was doubly difficult because Teemu's fiancée, Sirpa, was nine months pregnant.

While Jets supporters were crushed, Mighty Ducks fans were thrilled. Anaheim now had another elite player to ease the pressure on its lone superstar, 22-year-old Paul Kariya. Teemu played his first game with his new team on February 10, 1996, against the New York Islanders. He marked the occasion by scoring his 25th goal of the season, then went on to record points in his first 15 games for the Ducks, setting a club record.

Teemu missed one game during the streak when he flew to Winnipeg for the birth of his first child. On February 23, Sirpa gave birth to a baby boy named Eemil. Back in uniform two nights later, Teemu popped a hat trick against the San Jose Sharks. "I was so pumped," he admitted. "Before the game I was thinking about scoring a goal for Eemil."

Teemu gave the Mighty Ducks' power play more pizzazz.

Anaheim coach Ron Wilson was delighted with his new player. The Ducks' pitiful power play had suddenly become a menacing force. Opponents could no longer simply focus on stopping Kariya.

Prior to Teemu's arrival, Anaheim was 12 games under .500. In the 28 games after he joined the team, Anaheim was eight games over .500. If the Ducks had made the trade a few days earlier, they might have made the playoffs. They finished tied for eighth place in the conference with the Winnipeg Jets, but failed to qualify because they had one less win.

Teemu and Kariya tied for seventh in the NHL scoring derby with 108 points. Both were named as finalists for the Lady Byng Trophy as the league's most sportsmanlike player. Kariya won the award in a close vote. It was the first time in NHL history that two players on the same team had ever been nominated for the trophy.

As usual, Teemu returned to Finland after the season, but he didn't get much chance to relax. He played for Finland in two international tournaments: the World Championships in April and the World Cup in August. In July he also got married to Sirpa.

Teemu arrived at training camp in September 1996 in high spirits. He had adjusted to the idea of playing for a new team. As much as he liked Winnipeg, the warm California sunshine was hard to beat. And he had another reason to

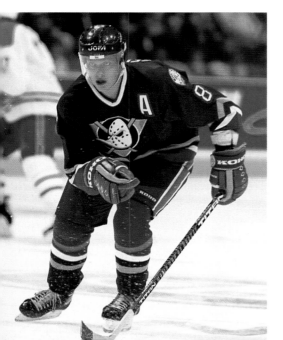

be happy: the Ducks had signed Jari Kurri, Teemu's former hockey idol and now one of his best friends.

Although Anaheim had to open the season without Paul Kariya, who was injured, Teemu got off to a fast start, scoring 10 points in his first six games. In a game against the Colorado Avalanche on October 10, he notched five points, including an amazing two goals and an assist in the last three minutes to help the Ducks rally for a 6–6 tie. It was the first time an Anaheim player had scored five points in a game.

But Teemu's impact went deeper than simply putting points on the board. His sunny personality also had a positive effect on the club. "Teemu is a great guy to have on the team when things get tense," says Steve Rucchin. "I'd say our attitude turned around 180 degrees when he got here. He truly has fun coming to the rink every day, and I think it's safe to say we all feel a little more at ease with him around."

Any doubts that Teemu was still bothered by his old leg injuries vanished in 1996–97. His line, with Kariya on left wing and Rucchin at center, became an explosive threat. They helped the Ducks achieve a franchise-high 85 points and place fourth in the Western Conference. Teemu posted 51 goals and 58 assists for 108 points, second only to Mario Lemieux in the scoring race. Kariya finished third with 99 points. The Ducks' deadly duo scored more points than any other pair of teammates in the NHL.

But more important, the Ducks made the playoffs for the first time in history. Ironically their opponent in the first round was the Phoenix Coyotes, Teemu's former team. The two clubs waged a bitter struggle. Anaheim won the first two games, but Phoenix roared back to take the

Sign of Greatness

Win or lose, Teemu Selanne always has time for hockey fans. Jack Ferreira, his former general manager with Anaheim, often tells the story about a frigid winter night in Calgary when the Ducks were getting on the team bus after a tough loss. About 50 fans, most of them children, were lined up behind a barricade. Teemu, who was wearing only a suit, went down the line, one by one, signing autographs and chatting until everyone had been taken care of.

next three. The sixth game went into overtime tied 2–2. In order to survive, the Ducks had to score the next goal. Midway through the first overtime period, Anaheim got a break. Teemu flipped a cross-ice pass through the neutral zone. The puck skipped over the stick of Coyotes defenseman Gerald Diduck, and Kariya alertly scooped it up. Streaking down the wing, he whipped a shot past goalie Nikolai Khabibulin. The crowd at Arrowhead Pond erupted in cheers.

Riding high on their momentum, the Ducks blanked Phoenix 3–0 in Game 7 and advanced to meet the Detroit Red Wings in the conference semifinal. This time, though, the Ducks came up a little short. The Red Wings swept the series, but the play was closer than the results would suggest. Three of the four games were decided in overtime. There was no shame in losing to Detroit, which went on to capture the Stanley Cup. As coach Ron Wilson pointed out: "We are going out with our heads high. We gave them everything we had."

THE DYNAMIC DUO

Teemu Selanne and his linemate Paul Kariya form one of the NHL's most dangerous scoring duos. Their explosive speed creates serious headaches for opposition defensemen. "When they take off, it's like they've got firecrackers up their backsides," says Colorado Avalanche defenseman Adam Foote. "No two guys can come out of the chute as quickly as them."

But though they share the same approach to hockey and are best friends off the ice, they are total opposites in personality. While Kariya is intense and serious and very protective of his privacy, Teemu is more outgoing and impulsive. "Paul likes to stay home and read his books. I get bored pretty easily when there's nothing to do," admits Teemu. "I'm always looking for fun."

After joining the Mighty

Ducks, Teemu lit up

Anaheim with his world-

class talent and his

sunny personality.

CHAPTER FIVE

Carrying the Load

The Mighty Ducks had to fly all the way to the other side of the planet to begin the 1997–98 season. Because the 1998 Winter Olympics were going to be held in Japan, the NHL decided to open its season with a pair of games in Tokyo between Anaheim and the Vancouver Canucks. The Canucks took the first game, and the Ducks, sparked by Teemu's two goals and an assist, won the second.

However, two notable faces—coach Ron Wilson and Paul Kariya—were missing from the Ducks' lineup. Wilson had been fired in the off-season and replaced with Pierre Pagé. Kariya, who was expected to attract a lot of attention in Tokyo because he is part Japanese, was a contract holdout. In Kariya's absence, Teemu was made captain. Not only was the Finn expected to provide team leadership, he was also counted on to carry the team's offense.

But without Kariya, Teemu had to change his style of play, which he found difficult. "With Paul, you knew if you'd find the open ice, the puck would come. He made it so easy. Without him, I have to find new ways to do damage."

After getting only one goal in his first seven games, Teemu caught fire, scoring 17 times in 11 straight games. The goal-scoring streak left him two games shy of the modern-day NHL record. His streak was snapped in the next game by the Montreal Canadiens on November 12. Even so, it's a day Teemu remembers fondly, because at 2:09 p.m. his wife Sirpa gave birth to their second son, Eetu.

Teemu wore the C when captain Paul Kariya was injured.

Teemu made it to the rink that evening, but after being up with Sirpa from 3:30 in the morning, he lacked his usual zip and failed to score as Anaheim lost 4–3. "I left my energy at the hospital," he admitted. "But it was a great day. I think my wife was the first star today."

Although other teams began assigning checkers to shut him down, Teemu continued to light the lamp. After 30 games, he had 23 goals, a third of the team's total output. No other Anaheim player had more than five.

On December 10, Kariya and the Ducks finally agreed on a new contract. The team got the news as it came off the ice after the first period of a game with the Pittsburgh Penguins. A minute later, Kariya picked up his phone in Vancouver and heard a huffing and puffing Teemu welcoming him back.

Kariya's return was a big boost for the team. In his first game back in uniform, the Selanne–Rucchin–Kariya line engineered all six goals as the Ducks beat the Washington Capitals 6–4.

By the time of the All-Star Game in February, Teemu led the league with 37 goals. Not surprisingly, he was voted to the first All-Star team. That year, however, the game had a new format. Instead of matching the Western Conference against the Eastern Conference, the game pitted North American All-Stars against the All-Stars from the rest of the world.

Of all the stars at this glamorous event, Teemu shone the brightest. In the shootout portion of the All-Star skills competition, he beat goalie Patrick Roy to score the winning goal for the World team. The next day at Vancouver's GM Place, playing on a line with fellow Finns Saku Koivu and Jere Lehtinen, he potted three goals in the big game.

The Godfather

When he was 18, Teemu Selanne made a goodwill visit to Helsinki Children's Hospital. Seeing all the sick kids left an impression. Soon after, he and a friend created the Godfathers Foundation, a group that raises funds for ailing children. Teemu donates most of the money he earns from his commercial endorsements to the cause. He also helps out with the NHL's Goals for Kids Foundation. Says Teemu: "Athletes are lucky, and it doesn't take so much for us to do these things. Once, a nurse told me that after we visit, the kids don't need painkillers for a week. That made me feel so good."

Although the North American team won 8–7, Teemu was voted the game's most valuable player, becoming the first European to win the award. His prize was a Dodge Durango truck. The vehicle boosted his car collection to a grand total of 24. "My wife's going to be mad," said Teemu, grinning impishly after the game. "I don't think she even knows how many cars I have."

The NHL shut down for two weeks after the All-Star Game to allow its players to compete at the Olympics. Most hockey experts felt the gold medal would be won by Canada, the United States or Sweden. Finland was a real underdog. But that suited Teemu, who noted: "I think it's a good situation. We have nothing to lose. Nobody expects us to win."

After advancing through the preliminary round, Finland faced its archrival Sweden in the medal round. The game was a scoreless tie midway through the third period when Teemu knifed through the Swedish defense to score on goalie Tommy Salo. The Finns added another goal and hung on to win 2–1.

The next game against Russia was a thriller. After Russia jumped into a 3–0 lead, Finland staged a frantic comeback, eventually tying the game 4–4 on a goal by Teemu. But the Finns couldn't

stop Pavel Bure, who scored five times to lead Russia to a 7–4 victory. Although they had lost a chance to play for gold, the Finns upset Canada 3–2 to win the bronze medal. "It was a great experience," says Teemu, who despite sitting out the last game with a pulled stomach muscle, tied with teammate Saku Koivu as the tournament's top scorer.

When the NHL season resumed, Teemu missed five games recovering from his injury. It was an injury Anaheim couldn't afford. Just before the Olympics, Kariya had suffered a serious concussion after being cross-checked in the head by Chicago's Gary Suter. Anaheim had hoped Kariya would recover quickly, but early in March, it was announced he would be sidelined for the rest of the season.

SHARPSHOOTERS

Many people think Teemu Selanne is the NHL's deadliest goal scorer. The statistics suggest they may be right. During the past three seasons, Teemu's goals-per-game average is easily the best in the league.

Player	Games	Goals	Average
Teemu Selanne	226	150	.664
John LeClair	240	144	.600
Peter Bondra	219	129	.589
Keith Tkachuk	218	128	.587
Paul Kariya	173	100	.578
Jaromir Jagr	221	126	.570
Pavel Bure	156	87	.558

(INCLUDES THE 1996–97, 1997–98 AND 1998–99 SEASONS)

Teemu returned in high gear, but Anaheim dropped out of playoff contention. The Flying Finn ended the season with 52 goals, tied with Washington's Peter Bondra for the most in the league.

Although Teemu's output was short of the 76 goals he racked up as a rookie, many thought he had an even more impressive season, considering the tighter defensive play in the NHL and his weak supporting cast. All told, Teemu's 52 goals represented 25 per cent of Anaheim's offense. Only one other modern-day player—Brett Hull of the 1990–91 St. Louis Blues—has ever scored a higher percentage of his team's goals.

Teemu was a runner-up for two postseason awards: the Hart Trophy as the NHL's most valuable player, which was won by Buffalo Sabres goalie Dominik Hasek, and the Lady Byng Trophy for the most sportsmanlike player, which went to Ron Francis of the Pittsburgh Penguins.

Teemu never gets tired of turning on the red light.

Winning one of the awards would have been nice, but Teemu admits that the trophy he most wants to get his hands on is the big one presented each year after the final playoff game. "The Stanley Cup is the thing I really want to win. It's my biggest dream."

Although Anaheim needs to add a few more skilled players to reach that lofty goal, in Teemu Selanne and Paul Kariya the club has two key parts of the puzzle. Teemu is optimistic the Ducks can find the missing pieces. "I am hoping," he says, "that the best things are still to come."

STATISTICS

National Hockey League (NHL)

Regular Season

Year	Team	GP	G	A	P	PIM
1992–93	Winnipeg	84	76	56	132	45
1993–94	Winnipeg	51	25	29	54	22
1994–95	Winnipeg	45	22	26	48	2
1995–96	Winnipeg	51	24	48	72	18
	Anaheim	28	16	20	36	4
1996–97	Anaheim	78	51	58	109	34
1997–98	Anaheim	73	52	34	86	30
1998–99	Anaheim	75	47	59	106	30
Totals		485	313	330	643	185

Playoffs

Year	Team	GP	G	A	P	PIM
1993	Winnipeg	6	4	2	6	2
1997	Anaheim	11	7	3	10	4
1999	Anaheim	4	2	2	4	2
Totals		21	13	7	20	8

Finnish Leagues

Regular Season

Year	Team	GP	G	A	P	PIM
1987–88	Jokerit 2	5	1	1	2	0
1988–89	Jokerit 2	34	35	33	68	12
1989–90	Jokerit 1	11	4	8	12	0
1990–91	Jokerit 1	42	33	25	58	12
1991–92	Jokerit 1	44	39	23	62	20
1994–95	Jokerit 1	20	7	12	19	6
Totals		156	119	102	221	50

Playoffs

Year	Team	GP	G	A	P	PIM
1989	Jokerit 2	5	7	3	10	4
1992	Jokerit 1	10	10	7	17	18
Totals		15	17	10	27	22

Finnish International Hockey

Year	Event	GP	G	A	P	PIM
1991	World Championships	10	6	5	11	2
1991	Canada Cup	6	1	1	2	2
1992	Olympics	8	7	4	11	6
1996	World Championships	6	5	3	8	0
1996	World Cup	4	3	2	5	0
1998	Olympics	5	4	6	10	8
Totals		39	26	21	47	18

Key

GP = Games Played   G = Goals   A = Assists
P = Points   PIM = Penalties in Minutes